MOLLY
MOVES TO
SESAME STREET

Featuring Jim Henson's Sesame Street Muppets

by JUDY FREUDBERG
Illustrated by JEAN CHANDLER

A SESAME STREET/GOLDEN PRESS BOOK

Published by Western Publishing Company, Inc.
in conjunction with Children's Television Workshop.

Molly stood on Sesame Street for the first time,
looking around at her new neighborhood. The movers
were carrying boxes and crates into her new apartment.
Nothing looked familiar.

"I wish we hadn't moved," thought Molly sadly.

Molly went inside where her mother was working. "Is this my new room?" she asked. Her mother nodded.

Molly stared at the bare walls. "It doesn't look like my room," she said.

"Don't worry, Molly. That's because your things aren't in it yet."

Molly's mother showed her what was inside the cardboard boxes.

"See?" she said. "Here are all your things, and when they are unpacked this will look like your own room."

Molly started taking her things out of one of the boxes and putting them away.

First Molly put away her collection of empty cereal boxes, lining them up neatly on the bookcase.

Then she put her miniature toy horses on her bedside table.

"Where are my marbles?" Molly wondered as she rummaged through a box.

"Oh, here they are,
right in the jar
where they belong."

Then she found the picture
she had drawn of her mother
and father, but she was too short
to hang it up over her bed.

"I'll hang the picture," said Molly's father.
"Why don't you go out and play?"

"I don't know where to go," said Molly.

"Just walk down Sesame Street, Molly," said her
mother. "I'm sure you'll find some friends. And by the
time you get back, we'll have everything put away."

So Molly went outside, excited about making new friends. As she walked along Sesame Street, she heard laughter coming from behind a fence. And somebody was counting out loud.

"18...19...Ah-ah-ah!...20! Here I come, ready or not!"

"What's going on?" wondered Molly as she came
to a play area.

Nobody was there! "That's strange," thought Molly.
"I know I heard voices!"

"Hey, is anybody here?" she yelled.

Big Bird popped out from behind the fence.
"Hello," said Molly. "I'm Molly and I just moved here."
"Oh boy!" exclaimed Big Bird. "A new neighbor on
Sesame Street. I'm Big Bird! Hey, everybody," he shouted.
"Come on out and meet Molly!"
Suddenly, Molly was surrounded by her new neighbors.

"Greetings!" said the Count. "I am the Count. Do you know why they call me the Count? Because I love to count things! One new neighbor! Ah-ah-ah-ah!"

"Me Cookie Monster," said Cookie Monster. "And me called Cookie Monster because me love cookies!"

"And do you know why they call me Ernie?" Ernie asked Molly. "Because that's my name! Hee-hee-hee!"

"Hello, Molly," said Bert, shaking her hand. "I'm very pleased to meet you."

"I am cute, adorable, furry old Grover," said Grover, peeking over Bert's shoulder. "Would you like to play hide-and-seek with us?"

"Sure!" exclaimed Molly. "And I'll be IT!"

So everyone hid while Molly counted to 20.

"Ready or not, here I come," called Molly. As she passed a trash can she heard a noise and lifted the lid of the can.

"Gotcha!" said Molly. She tagged Oscar.

"Hey!" yelled Oscar. "Cut it out! I'm not playing any dumb game. Don't bother me!"

He slammed down the lid of his can.

Ernie's voice came from his hiding place. "Don't pay any attention to him, Molly. That's just Oscar, our neighborhood grouch."

"I can be pretty grouchy myself sometimes," said
Molly. She banged on Oscar's can. "Oscar, I wouldn't play
with you if you were the last grouch on earth."

"Hey," said Oscar, opening the lid of the can
again, "I couldn't have said that better myself. This is the
beginning of a terrible friendship!"

Then everyone came out of hiding.

"Come on, Molly," said Big Bird. "Let's all go to
Mr. Hooper's store for a snack."

"So you're our new neighbor," said Mr. Hooper
when he met Molly. "I hope you'll like it here with us
on Sesame Street."

"Oh, I already do!" she exclaimed.

"Uh, Molly," said Bert, sipping his water, "would you
like to come over and see my paper clip collection?"

"And my great set of drums!" cried Ernie.

"Let me ask my mother," said Molly. "I'll be right back."

Molly was surprised when she saw her new room.
"Wow!" she exclaimed. "This really does look like
my room! And it almost feels like it, too. May I ask
my friends over to see it?"

"Of course you may," answered her parents.

Molly went out on her front stoop
and called to her new friends.
"Hey! Ernie, Bert, Big Bird, Grover,
everybody! Come and see my new room!"
And they all hurried to Molly's new house.

"Oh, my," said Bert, "you collect cereal boxes!"

"And miniature horses!" exclaimed Ernie.

Big Bird admired Molly's drawing of her mother and father, while the Count began counting Molly's marble collection.

Oscar popped up from the cardboard boxes. "You've got great taste in furniture!" he said.

Molly looked around at all of her new friends in her new room and smiled. "Now it feels like my room," she cried happily, "and I feel right at home!"